Contents

Dates: in this book, dates are followed by the letters BCE (Before Common Era) or CE (Common Era). This is instead of using BC (Before Christ) and AD (*Anno Domini*, meaning in the year of our Lord). The date numbers are the same in both systems.

Introducing Judaism

Judaism is one of the oldest religions in the world. It involves beliefs and ways of life that have been important to its followers for over 4000 years. This book tells you about Jewish culture and beliefs.

Generally, a Jew is a person whose mother was Jewish, or someone who has decided to become a follower of the Jewish religion. Not everyone who is born Jewish follows the religion. Not all Jews who do follow the religion follow it in the same way. However, most Jews feel that their background and what they share with other Jews is very important.

One way of describing this is to say that the Jews think of themselves as being like a large family. In any family, different members may have different opinions and work in different ways, but the fact that they are a family is something that runs through all their lives. Today, Jews live in many different parts of the world, but most Jews feel that they have something in common with other Jews. This is true even if they live far away and in countries where everyday life is quite different.

▲ A Jewish family in Jerusalem.

What are Jewish beliefs?

Jews believe that there is one God. They believe that this God is a spirit who is **eternal**. This means he was never born and will never die. He has always existed and always will exist. They believe that he made the world and everything in it, and he loves and cares about what he made. He is so holy that his name cannot be used, but Jews usually call him **Adonai**, which means 'Lord'. Jews use any name of God with great respect and would never use it carelessly or as a swear word. To show how important they think it is, many Jews avoid even writing the word God. This is why in some Jewish books you sometimes see it written 'G-d'.

Judaism

Sue Penney

Heinemann
LIBRARY

www.heinemann.co.uk
Visit our website to find out more information about Heinemann Library books.

To order:
☎ Phone 44 (0) 1865 888066
📄 Send a fax to 44 (0) 1865 314091
💻 Visit the Heinemann Bookshop at www.heinemann.co.uk to browse our catalogue
and order online.

First published in Great Britain by Heinemann Library, Halley Court, Jordan Hill, Oxford OX2 8EJ
a division of Reed Educational and Professional Publishing Ltd.
Heinemann is a registered trademark of Reed Educational & Professional Publishing Ltd.

OXFORD MELBOURNE AUCKLAND JOHANNESBURG BLANTYRE
GABORONE IBADAN PORTSMOUTH (NH) USA CHICAGO

Designed by Ken Vail Graphic Design
Originated by Universal
Printed by Wing King Tong in Hong Kong.

ISBN 0 431 09314 8 (hardback)   ISBN 0 431 09321 0 (paperback)
05 04 03 02 01   05 04 03 02 01
10 9 8 7 6 5 4 3 2   10 9 8 7 6 5 4 3 2

British Library Cataloguing in Publication Data

Penney, Sue
Judaism. – (World Beliefs and Cultures)
1.Judaism – Juvenile literature
1.Title
296

Acknowledgements
The Publishers would like to thank the following for permission to reproduce photographs:
AKG/Erich Lessing p. 9; Ancient Art and Architecture p. 24; Andes Press Agency/Carlos Reyes-Manzo p. 26a;
Carlos Reyes-Manzo, Andes Press Agency pp. 39, 42; Circa Photo Library pp. 16, 28, /Barrie Searle pp. 7, 12,
22, 37, /John Smith p. 15, /Zbigniew Kosc p. 41; Collections/ Mike Kipling p. 10; Impact Photos /Robin
Laurance p. 23, /Rachel Morton p 13, /Steward Weir p. 20; John T. Hopf p.25; Juliette Soester pp. 5, 18, 30,
34, 36; Peter Osborne, p. 29; Photoedit pp. 19, 35, 43; The Stock Market pp.17, 21; Topham Picturepoint
p. 11; Zev Radovan pp 4, 6, 14, 26b, 27, 31, 32.

Cover photograph reproduced with permission of AKG.

Our thanks to Philip Emmett for his comments in the preparation of this book.

Every effort has been made to contact copyright holders of any material reproduced in this book.
Any omissions will be rectified in subsequent printings if notice is given to the Publisher.

Words appearing in the text in bold, **like this**, are explained in the Glossary.

The Covenant

Jews believe that they have a special relationship with God. They are often called the Chosen People. This is because of the **Covenant** which God made with the Jews. A covenant is a solemn agreement. This agreement was that Jews would follow the laws that God gave. In return, he would look after them. The fact that they believe they are a Chosen People does not mean that Jews expect an easy life. It means that they believe they have a greater duty and responsibility to worship God and to live in the right way. They believe that God loves human beings, and it is the duty of human beings to love God in return. They believe that this love can be shown by following the instructions that God gave to show people how to live, and by worshipping him. Jews believe that these instructions are collected together in the **Torah**. Torah means Books of Teaching. Jews believe that the books of the Torah are very important.

▼ *Young Jews outside a London synagogue.*

Judaism fact check

- Judaism began about 4000 years ago.
- Jews worship one God whom they often call Adonai.
- The Jewish place of worship is called a synagogue.
- The most important Jewish holy books are called the Torah, which are usually written on **scrolls** for use in the synagogue.
- The Torah is written in **Hebrew**. Modern Hebrew is the official language of Israel.
- There are two symbols most often used for Judaism. One is a six-pointed star, called the Star of David or the Magen David (Shield of David). The other symbol is a candlestick with seven branches called a **menorah**.
- There are just over 13 million Jews in the world today.
  - ♦ About 5.8 million Jews live in the USA.
  - ♦ About 4.8 million Jews live in Israel.
  - ♦ About 1.2 million Jews live in Europe, of whom about 300,000 live in the UK.
  - ♦ About 550,000 Jews live in Russia.
  - ♦ There are small Jewish populations in many other countries, including about 100,000 in Australia and 120,000 in Africa.

Abraham and Moses

Judaism began so long ago that no one really knows how it began. Jews believe that two men were most important in shaping the religion and working out the early beliefs. The first of these men was called Abram, later called Abraham. The second was called Moses.

Abraham

Jews call Abraham *Avraham Avinu*, which in **Hebrew** means 'our father Abraham'. He lived about 4000 years ago, in a city called Ur, in modern Iraq. Today, the site of the city has been excavated by archaeologists and is called Tall al Maqayyar. In the days of Abraham, Ur was an important city on the banks of the River Euphrates. It was especially important as a centre of worship for the moon god Nanna.

You can find the places mentioned in this book on the map on page 44.

The stories about Abraham were passed down from father to son for hundreds of years before they were written down. This means that we cannot be sure of the details about his life. However, it seems that Abraham was rich and respected, but that he found there were things in his life that did not make him happy. The worship of the moon god and other statues worried him greatly. He seems to have been the first person to act on a belief that there was a greater God, who should be worshipped. Guided by his feelings about this God, Abraham and his family left Ur and set out on a journey which he felt was led by the God he worshipped.

Many people who lived in this part of the world were, and still are, nomads. Nomads do not have a fixed home, but live in tents. They move these from place to place, usually depending on where their animals can find water in the desert. From this point of view, Abraham's journey was not so unusual. Jews believe that what made it different was that Abraham believed that God was guiding him, and was looking after him.

▲ *Abraham and his family travelled from Ur to Canaan through areas which must have looked similar to this picture of Mount Sinai today.*

Moses

Jews call Moses *Moshe Rabbenu*, which means 'our teacher Moses'. He lived about 500 years after the time of Abraham. At that time, Jews had been slaves in Egypt for many years, and were being treated very badly. Moses came to believe that God wanted him to rescue the Jews. He went to see the **Pharaoh** (king of Egypt) and told him that if the Jews were not freed, disasters would happen. The Pharaoh did not want to lose the slaves who were working for him, so he refused.

The ten plagues

According to the Jewish holy books, ten disasters called plagues then hit the country. Rivers turned to blood, and there were plagues of frogs, lice and flies. All the farm animals died, then all the people developed boils. The seventh plague was hailstorms, and this was followed by a plague of locusts. Then there was darkness and the sun did not shine. The last plague was the death of the eldest son in every Egyptian family. Today, many people would believe that these were natural disasters, but everyone involved then believed that the plagues had been sent by God as a punishment. After the death of the boys, the Pharaoh just wanted to get rid of the Jews, and so he allowed them to leave. They were led by Moses to the country called Canaan, which is in the area that today we call Israel.

▲ *Most synagogues have the first words of each of the Ten Commandments on a plaque above the Ark.*

The Ten Commandments

A commandment is an important rule. Jews believe that the Ten Commandments were given to Moses by God. They are the basis of the Jewish religion and include basic laws which are followed by almost all human beings. They can be summed up like this:

1 I am the Lord your God. You must not have any other gods but me.

2 You must not make any **idols** to worship.

3 You must not use God's name carelessly.

4 You must remember to keep the **Sabbath** day holy.

5 You must respect your father and your mother.

6 You must not murder.

7 You must not commit **adultery**.

8 You must not steal.

9 You must not tell lies about other people.

10 You must not **covet**.

Jewish history – the early days

This map shows how the land was divided among the twelve tribes of Israel.

Map labels:
Mediterranean Sea
ASHER
NAPHTALI
ZEBULUN
Sea of Galilee
ISSACHAR
MANASSEH
River Jordan
GAD
EPHRAIM
DAN
BENJAMIN
JUDAH
Dead Sea
REUBEN
SIMEON
N
0   50 km
0   50 miles

The beginning

Jewish history is found mainly in the Jewish holy books, put together over hundreds of years. The writers' main interest was the relationship between God and the Jewish people, so the books are not like a modern history book. This is the story of the Jewish people as it is found in their holy books. In the early days, the Jews were called **Israelites**.

Jews believe that God led Abraham to a country which he gave to Abraham and his descendants for ever. This country was on the shores of the Mediterranean Sea, and it included the area that today we call Israel. Abraham's family lived there until the time of his grandson, Jacob, when a severe famine hit the area. In order to find food, they went to Egypt, where they settled. Some years later, there was a revolution in Egypt, and a new **Pharaoh** came to the throne. He felt that there was a danger in having a large number of foreigners following their own way of life within his country, and he made them into slaves. Several generations of Israelites lived like this, until the time of Moses, who rescued them. These are the events that Jews remember at the festival of Passover. The Israelites then became nomads in the desert for about 40 years, until they reached the country called Canaan. Moses died when they were within sight of the country, and the new leader, Joshua, led the people in.

Judges

Other tribes were settled in Canaan, and the Israelites had several years of war before they gained control. Then the land was divided up among twelve groups, who are known as the Twelve Tribes of Israel. Each tribe had an area of land of its own. The most important leaders of these tribes were called **Judges**. When there was a problem – usually an enemy attacking one tribe – the Judges could call on other Judges to bring members of their tribe to help. However, it was difficult for the Israelites to be united. The last Judge was a great man called Samuel. The Israelites asked Samuel to choose a king for them, who could rule over all the Israelites and so make them stronger in battle. Samuel chose a man named Saul.

Kings

Saul was king for about 40 years before he was killed in battle. The next king was David. He is probably best remembered for the story about how, as a young boy, he fought a giant named Goliath. Even though he was only young, he outwitted the giant and killed him with a stone from his sling. As king, David was very successful, and many Jews still look back to the days of King David as the best time in their history. When he died his son Solomon took over. The country was peaceful and rich, and a magnificent new **Temple** was built so that God could be worshipped in a suitable way.

Israel and Judah

After the death of Solomon, the country divided. The northern tribes broke away to make a separate country called Israel. The southern tribes formed the country of Judah. The people who lived there became known as the Jews.

After about 200 years, in 722 BCE, Israel was conquered by the Assyrians, who were a great power at the time. Many of the people were taken away to live in Assyria. About a hundred years later, in 586 BCE, soldiers from Babylon took over the southern kingdom of Judah. Many of the people were taken to live in Babylon. When Cyrus the Great of Persia conquered Babylon in 538 BCE, he allowed all the people who had been taken there by the Babylonians to return to their home country if they wished. Some Jews chose to return to Judah, but most chose to stay in Babylon.

▼ A reconstruction of the Ishtar Gate – the main entrance into Babylon at the time the Jews lived there.

The Diaspora

The **Diaspora** is the name given to Jews living in countries other than Israel. It comes from a word that means dispersed or scattered. The Diaspora began around the time that the Babylonians invaded Judah. Apart from the Jews who were made to leave their country to live in Babylon, other Jews chose to go and live in other countries rather than be ruled by an enemy. This has happened many times in the Jews' history. This is one reason why today there are Jews living in many countries of the world.

Recent Jewish history

▲ *In the Middle Ages, life was difficult for Jews. In 1190, 150 Jews died in this castle in York, England.*

Background

For much of their history, Jews have had to fight to keep their identity. Rulers took over their country and put pressure on them to give up their Jewish ways. The Romans took over their country (then called Palestine) in 63 BCE. A hundred years later, the Romans crushed a revolt by a group of Jews. As part of this, in 70 CE, the **Temple** – the most important place of worship for Jews – was destroyed. This was a very important event in Jewish history, and Jews today still pray that one day the Temple will be rebuilt. The one wall which remains is a very important site for Jews to visit.

After this revolt, many Jews left Palestine and joined other Jews who were part of the **Diaspora** (Jews living in other countries). For hundreds of years, life for many Jews was very difficult. Jews were banned from living in many countries. In other countries they were forced to live in ghettos – areas of a town which were often walled so that the Jews could be locked in at night. They were treated as if they were not as good as other people. Christians said that Jews were responsible for killing Jesus, and in countries which were mainly Christian, Jews were persecuted because of this.

The Holocaust

In the early years of the twentieth century, there were enormous economic problems in many countries. Germany suffered particular problems because of the crippling conditions that were placed on it at the end of World War I. When the **Nazis** came to power, they wanted to make Germany a great and powerful country again. It was convenient to find a group to blame for all the problems. The Nazi leader, Adolf Hitler, hated Jews, and he began a campaign to get rid of them. First, all Jews had to register at a local office. Then they had to wear a yellow Star of David on their clothes so they could be seen and identified. Gradually, all their rights were taken away – they were not allowed to own cars, businesses had to close, children were not allowed to go to school. Life became harder and harder.

Then the Nazis decided they had found what they called the 'final solution to the Jewish problem'. This was to get rid of all Jews in the world. Jews were rounded up and sent to special **concentration camps**. Many were killed immediately, others were starved, beaten and tortured. By the end of World War II, six million Jews were dead, one and a half million of them children. One in three of the world's Jewish population had been killed. This time of terrible persecution became known as the **Holocaust**.

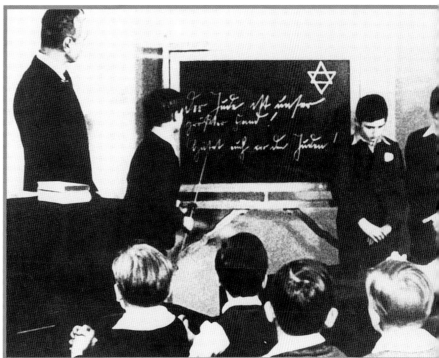

▲ *Life in Nazi Germany. Two Jewish boys stand at the front, while the class reads from the blackboard 'The Jew is our greatest enemy. Beware of the Jew!'*

After the war

The state of Israel was established in 1948. Its law states that any Jew has the right to live in Israel if they wish to. Almost immediately after it had been established, Israel was at war with its neighbours, because Arabs who were living in the area that had been given to Jews did not want the state of Israel to exist. During the next 50 years, there were several wars between Jews and Arabs, and bombings and terrorist attacks were frequent. In the last years of the twentieth century, changing attitudes and several interventions by successive US presidents led to some improvements in relations. Israel signed peace treaties with Egypt (1979) and Jordan (1994).

Anne Frank

Anne Frank was the daughter of a Jewish family who were living in Holland when it was taken over by the Germans in 1940. In July 1942, the family went into hiding, and for over two years lived in a 'Secret Annexe' behind the warehouse which her father had owned. In August 1944, they were betrayed and caught. They were taken to concentration camps and Anne, her sister and her mother all died. During their time in the Secret Annexe, Anne kept a diary. When they were taken away, the diary was rescued, and after the war ended, it was published by Anne's father. It has become a best-seller all over the world. The house where they lived is now a museum, and the Anne Frank House and other charities work to try to educate people towards the end of racism and persecution.

The different groups of Jews

▲ *An Orthodox Jew, dressed for worship.*

In any religion, different individuals have different opinions. The followers of Judaism do not agree about everything. They are all individuals, and what is very important to one may be less important to another. They all share the most important beliefs, but the way in which those beliefs affect their lives is not the same for everyone. There are two main groups of Jews today – **Orthodox** Jews and **Progressive** Jews. Orthodox Jews do not agree with some of the teachings of Progressive Jews.

Orthodox Jews

In the world today, more Jews belong to the Orthodox tradition than to any of the other groups.

Orthodox Jews believe that the **Torah** is the word of God. They believe that it teaches how God wants people to live, and that it will never change. They believe that the teaching stays the same, even though at different times it will be applied in different ways. This means that no matter when or where they live, people will always know what God wants for them.

Both at home and in the synagogue, Orthodox Jews are more likely to follow strictly all the laws of the Torah. In the synagogue, men and women sit separately, and women do not take part in the service. At weekday morning services men wear the traditional **tefillin** (small leather boxes) as well as the skullcap (or a hat) and prayer robe which most Jewish men wear.

The Hasidic Movement

The **Hasidic** movement is one of the most important groups of Orthodox Jews. It began in Poland in the seventeenth century. Thousands of Hasidic Jews were killed in the **Holocaust**, and many of those who were left moved to other countries in Europe or to the USA or Israel. Today, there are Hasidic communities in many cities, including Jerusalem, London, New York and Melbourne. They emphasize trusting in God, reading the holy books and observing the **Sabbath**. They have their own schools and synagogues, and many Hasidic Jews still wear traditional Polish clothes. The men wear beards and sidelocks and dress in black. They keep their heads covered at all times. The women dress modestly, with long skirts and long sleeves.

Progressive Jews

In the Progressive group there are several other smaller groups. Probably the largest are the **Reform** and **Liberal** movements. Of course, even within these groups, not everyone thinks in exactly the same way.

Reform and Liberal Jews

Reform and Liberal Jews share the belief that Judaism can change to suit different circumstances. The Reform movement began in Germany during the nineteenth century. It teaches that it is not necessary to obey all the laws of the Torah, and that laws can be changed or ignored if they are no longer appropriate. Generally, the changes make it easier for Jews to live among people who do not share their religion.

Liberal Judaism began in London in the early years of the twentieth century. It grew from the idea that Reform Judaism had not gone far enough. Liberal Jews teach that each person should decide for themselves how they are going to follow the religion. They believe that God will guide their decisions, and that what is right for one person may not be right for another.

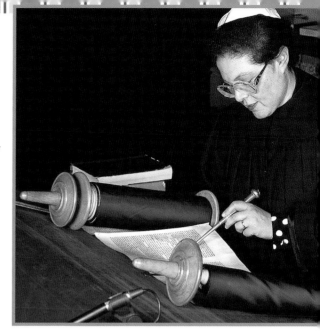

▲ *In Progressive Judaism, women can become Rabbis. This is Rabbi Tabbick in a Reform Synagogue in London.*

Orthodox Jews

In the synagogue

- Men always wear special clothes for worship
- Women sit in a separate gallery
- Men always lead the worship, only men may become **rabbis**
- Services always use the **Hebrew** language
- **Bar mitzvah** held for boys at 13, different service for girls
- Musical instruments never used

At home

- Sabbath is kept as a day of total rest
- Rules about **kosher** food kept very strictly
- Festivals follow the traditional observances
- Someone is counted as Jewish only if their mother was.

Progressive Jews

In the synagogue

- Men may wear a skullcap, but do not usually wear special clothes
- Men and women sit together
- Men and women lead worship, women can become rabbis
- Services usually held in everyday language
- Same services held for boys and girls at 13
- Musical instruments sometimes used

At home

- Sabbath is a day not to attend paid work
- Rules about kosher food may not be strictly observed
- Some **fasts** are not observed, Sabbath and festivals do not always begin at sunset
- Someone is Jewish if either parent was, or if they were brought up as a Jew.

Jewish holy books

Jews are sometimes called the People of the Book, and their holy books are very important to their life and their religion. The complete Scriptures are called the **Tenakh**. They are divided into three sections. The first is the **Torah**, the Books of Teaching. The second is the **Nevi'im**, the Books of the Prophets. The third is the **Ketuvim**, the Books of Writings. Putting the first letters of these three Hebrew words together – T, N, K – gives the word Tenakh.

The Torah

The five books of the Torah are **Genesis**, **Exodus**, **Leviticus**, **Numbers** and **Deuteronomy**. They are sometimes known as the Five Books of Moses. The books are the history of the beginning of the Jewish people, and Jews believe that they contain instructions about how God wants them to live. Jews call these instructions **mitzvot**, which means commandments. Jewish tradition says that there are 613 mitzvot. 248 mitzvot are things that Jews are commanded to do, such as honouring parents and keeping the **Sabbath**. The other 365 mitzvot are things that Jews are commanded not to do, such as stealing and murdering. Some Jews keep the mitzvot very strictly.

Sefer Torah

An open scroll of the Torah, showing how it is wound onto rollers.

For reading in the synagogue, the Torah is written in columns, on scrolls. A scroll is like a book with one long page wound around a wooden roller at each end. A full-size scroll is about 60 metres long when it is unwound. A scroll of the Torah is called a **Sefer Torah**. Every copy is written by hand, by a scribe who has been specially trained. He uses special ink and a quill pen. A Sefer Torah takes over a year to complete.

The material used for a scroll is **parchment**, not paper. Parchment is animal skin that has been specially treated and smoothed so that it can be written on. Many scrolls used in synagogues are very old and valuable. All scrolls are treated with very great care, and the parchment is never touched by hands. A special pointer called a **yad** is used to follow the words as the scroll is read in the synagogue. If the text became smudged or damaged, the scroll could not be used.

The Nevi'im

The **Nevi'im** is a collection of history books. It includes the teachings of the **prophets**. All through Jewish history there have been men and women who felt that they were inspired by God to give messages to the Jews. Sometimes their messages grew out of a particular situation, but Jews believe that much of what they taught still has meaning today. Three of the most important prophets were Elijah, Isaiah and Jeremiah, but there are many others.

Some of the books of the Nevi'im are read in the services in the synagogue. They are not usually written on scrolls. Others are not read in services, but Jews may read them at home.

The Ketuvim

Ketuvim means writings, and the books include many different types of writing. Many of the books are stories from the history of the Jews. The book that is used most often, in the synagogue and at home, is the Book of **Psalms**. A psalm is a sort of poem, and it can be used like a religious song. Many of the Psalms are supposed to have been written by King David. Some of the other books of the Ketuvim are read at particular festivals.

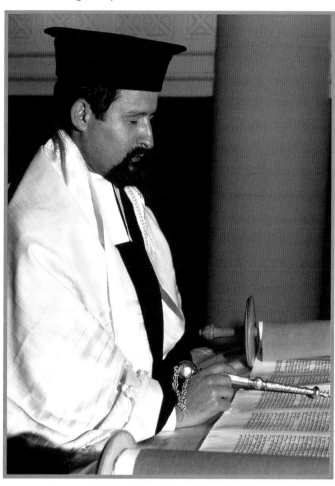

▼ *Reading the Torah in the synagogue, using the yad to follow the words.*

Other writings

As well as the Tenakh, there are other writings of great importance to Jews. For hundreds of years, the leaders of Judaism handed down oral (spoken) traditions about the mitzvot, explaining how they were to be kept – for example, defining the word 'work' for the command not to work on the Sabbath.

By 200 CE, Jews were scattering around the Roman Empire because of ill treatment. A Jewish leader and **rabbi** at this time saw that it was necessary to write down the oral traditions so that different Jewish groups did not grow apart. This written record was called the **Mishnah**. The Mishnah was studied by Jews, especially in Israel and Babylon, and their discussions about it were carefully written down. About 500 CE, these discussions were collected together and organized. Each paragraph of the Mishnah was written down, with the discussions and comments next to it. This collection is called the **Talmud**. The Talmud is very important for Jews today, and is still studied carefully by Jewish scholars.

What the holy books say

The holy books of Judaism contain thousands of years of history, stories, rules and instructions. They have been known and loved by Jews for over 4000 years. Here are some 'snapshots' of what they contain.

The creation

The book of **Genesis** begins with the story of the creation of the world. It says that for six days God commanded things to happen. These commands brought the world as we know it into being.

God commanded:

Day 1: light and dark, day and night
Day 2: earth's atmosphere ('a dome over the earth')
Day 3: the land to divide from the sea, and plants to grow on the land
Day 4: sun, moon and stars, and so days, years and seasons
Day 5: sea creatures and birds
Day 6: land animals and human beings.

On the seventh day God rested because creation was finished and '*he saw that it was good*'. It is because of this that Jews rest on the seventh day, Saturday, which they call the **Sabbath**.

The Shema

The Shema (pronounced to rhyme with afar) is the most important Jewish prayer. Jews say the Shema when they get up in the morning, and before they go to bed at night. It is recited as part of the morning and evening services in the synagogue. It is also said by a Jew who is dying, if they are able to speak. If not, it is repeated by the relatives at the bedside. This is what the Shema says:

▲ *This scribe is writing on a **mezuzah** scroll, using a special quill pen. A mezuzah contains the first two paragraphs of the Shema.*

Hear, Israel, the Lord is our God, the Lord is one. Now you must love the Lord your God with all your heart, and with all your soul and with all your strength. And these words, which I am commanding you today, shall be upon your heart. And you shall teach them carefully to your children, and speak of them when you are sitting in your house, when you are walking along the road, when you lie down and when you rise up. And you must bind them as a sign upon your arm, and they shall be a token between your eyes. And you must write them on the doorposts of your house and on your gates. (Deuteronomy 6: 4–9)

The Prophets

There are 21 Books of Prophets in the **Nevi'im**. Stories and teaching from other **prophets** are also found in the **Torah**. Some of the books are very long. For example, the Book of Isaiah has 60 chapters. Others are very short, and contain only a few chapters. Here are a few examples of what the prophets say.

No longer shall you need the sun for light by day, nor the shining of the moon by night, for the Lord shall be your light everlasting, your God shall be your glory. Your sun shall set no more, your moon no more withdraw, for the Lord shall be a light to you for ever and your days of mourning shall be ended. (Isaiah 60: 19–20)

This is what the Lord asks of you: only to do justice and to love mercy and to walk humbly with your God. (Micah 6: 8)

The word of the Lord came to me, as follows, 'Before I formed you in the womb, I knew you, and before you were born I made you holy – I have appointed you to be a prophet to the nations.' But I said, 'But, Lord God, look, I do not know how to speak, for I am still young.' Then the Lord said to me, 'Do not say "I am still young", for everywhere I will send you, you will go, and everything I command you, you will speak. Do not be afraid, for I am with you to take care of you.' (Jeremiah 1: 4–8)

They shall beat their swords into ploughshares and their spears into pruning hooks. Nation shall not lift up sword against nation, nor shall they practise for war any more. (Isaiah 2: 4)

These words of peace from Isaiah 2: 4 were thought to be so fitting that they are carved on the wall of the United Nations Building in New York. (The United Nations is an international organization formed in 1945 to try to encourage countries to work peacefully together.)

▼ *The United Nations building in New York.*

Worship at home

The way Jews live is a very important part of their belief. They believe that life itself was given by God, so even ordinary everyday things like preparing a meal or going to bed should include God, and are ways in which they can worship him.

▲ *A mezuzah is always attached to the right-hand doorpost.*

Mezuzah

The **mezuzah** is a tiny scroll made of **parchment**. On it are written the first two paragraphs of the Shema, the most important Jewish prayer. This scroll is usually covered with a special case made of wood, plastic or metal, then attached to the right-hand side of the doorpost. Mezuzot (the plural of mezuzah) can be attached to the doorway of every room except those of the bathroom and toilet, which are not thought suitable places for a holy object. Jews touch the mezuzah on their way in and out of the room, as a way of reminding themselves that God is always there. It also reminds them of God's promise that 'you are blessed when you come in and blessed when you go out' (Deuteronomy 28:6).

Daily worship

Jews may pray at any time. There are special prayers for getting up in the morning and before going to bed, and before and after food. They show that God is at the centre of Jews' lives. Jewish men wear a **kippah**, a skullcap, for synagogue worship, and some men wear it all the time. Covering the head like this is a sign of the person's respect for God. **Orthodox** Jewish men also wear a **tallit katan** under their other clothes. This is rectangular, usually made of wool, and is worn over the shoulders with a hole for the head to go through. It has fringes at each end. (This is not the same as the much larger tallit, properly called a **tallit gadol**, which Jewish men wear for some services in the synagogue.)

Sabbath in the home

Sabbath (in **Hebrew** Shabbat) is the Jewish day of rest and worship. It begins at sunset on Friday and lasts until sunset on Saturday. All Jewish days are counted from sunset to sunset because in Genesis it says 'Evening passed and morning came – that was the first day' (Genesis 1:5). During Friday the house is cleaned and tidied, and the Sabbath eve meal is prepared. The Sabbath begins when the wife or mother of the family lights two candles and says a prayer which welcomes the Sabbath.

After the synagogue service on the Friday evening, the family eat the Sabbath eve meal. This is the most important meal of the week, and it is always the best the family can afford. It always includes two loaves of **challah bread**. The meal is a chance for the family to be together and is a relaxed and happy occasion.

Keeping the Sabbath

On the Sabbath, Jews remember that in the story of creation, God made the world in six days and rested on the seventh day. So on this day, Jews do no work. For strict Orthodox Jews, this does not just mean their job. It means not doing anything which is classed as work. This includes cooking (food is prepared the day before), driving a car, shopping and so on. It makes the day one in which they can relax at home or with friends, without rushing around doing chores. The Sabbath ends with the **Havdalah** ceremony, when there are prayers and a special plaited candle is lit. Everyone smells a box of spices, and hopes that the peace of the Sabbath will spread through the coming week, just as the smell of the spices spreads through the house.

▲ *Lighting the Sabbath candles means that the Sabbath has begun.*

Jonathan's view

Jonathan is 13 and comes from an Orthodox Jewish family who live in Leeds.

I enjoy Shabbat, because it is a special day. Sometimes we call it Queen Shabbat to show how special it is. I always get quite excited on a Friday. In winter, school finishes so that we can get home before it is dark. The house is ready and then Mum lights the candles and says the prayer that means Shabbat has begun. I really like the idea that what we are doing is what Jews have done for thousands of years, and are still doing all over the world. It makes me feel a part of a really important tradition. I know some people who aren't Jewish think it must be a very boring day, but it isn't – it's a day for enjoying yourself quietly and getting ready for a busy week.

Worship in the synagogue

Jews believe that they can worship God anywhere. But like most religions they have special places where they meet for worship, and these are called synagogues. Jews do not usually use the word synagogue. Many Jews call it **shul** (rhymes with rule), some use the name Bet ha Knesset, which means 'place of meeting'. **Reform** Jews call it the **Temple**. It is likely that synagogues began when the Jews had been taken away to Babylon after the destruction of Jerusalem in 586 BCE. They began meeting in each other's houses so that they could pray and study the holy books together. Then special buildings were used which could be set aside for Jews to meet for both worship and study.

When Jews enter a synagogue they wash their hands. This is to make them fit to worship God. Then they say a prayer which thanks God that they can worship him. Part of the prayer says:

> I will worship facing towards your holy Temple. Lord, I love the dwelling of your house and the place where your glory rests. I will worship and bow and bend my knee before the Lord my maker.

A full synagogue service cannot take place unless there is a **minyan** – a group of ten adult men – present. If there are fewer than ten men present, the service can still go ahead, but some of the prayers are omitted.

▼ *Orthodox Jewish men wear special clothes at most services.*

Special clothes

In Orthodox synagogues, men wear special clothes for worship. They wear the **kippah**, which many Jewish men wear all the time. They also wear a special robe, called a **tallit**, over their other clothes. This is usually rectangular, and can be made of any natural fibre, though wool or silk are used most often. A full-sized tallit measures about 2 metres by 1.5 metres. It has a fringe and tassels at each end. These are there because the **Torah** tells Jews to put tassels on their clothes to help them remember God's commandments (Numbers 15: 39).

For weekday services in Orthodox synagogues, men also wear two small leather boxes. These are called **tefillin** (one is called a **tefillah**). They contain small pieces of **parchment**, which have the first two paragraphs of the Shema written on them. The boxes have long straps attached to them. One box is worn on the upper part of the left arm (right arm for a left-handed person). It is placed so that when the arm is resting, the box points towards the heart. This reminds Jews that it is important to love God. The other box is worn so

▲ *A rabbi inspecting the scroll from a tefillah.*

that it is in the centre of the forehead, just above where the hair starts to grow. This reminds Jews that they must love and serve God with their mind. Orthodox Jewish men may wear tefillin for prayers at home, too.

Caring for tefillin

Like **mezuzot**, tefillin are very important objects for Jews. Both mezuzot and tefillin can only be written by a trained scribe using special materials. They must be opened and checked by a **rabbi** about once every three years to make sure that the writing has not faded. If it is undamaged, the writing can be written over. If the parchment has cracked, it must be replaced. Jews always handle mezuzot and tefillin with great care and respect.

Rabbis

Rabbi is a **Hebrew** word that means 'master' or 'teacher' – in other words, a respected leader. Rabbis are the leaders of Jewish communities. They are respected because they have studied the Torah and other Scriptures, and know a great deal about Jewish law. In the synagogue, the rabbi often leads the prayers, and may give an address during the service. A rabbi also conducts wedding and funeral services. Many rabbis help to lead classes, educating members of the Jewish community about Judaism and helping them to learn more about the Torah.

Rabbis are often asked to make decisions about Jewish law – for example, about whether or not a particular item of food is **kosher** and therefore fit for Jews to eat. Three rabbis together form a **bet din**, which is a Jewish court. These courts are important in deciding matters of Jewish law, and they also issue the **get**, the certificate of Jewish divorce. It is a bet din that organizes matters when a person wishes to **convert** to Judaism. In the Jewish community, rabbis are often asked for their advice because they are so respected by the people. Some are marriage guidance counsellors, some are chaplains to hospitals or prisons so that they can help to look after any Jews who are there.

Synagogues

Like any building, synagogues reflect the time when they were built, and the attitudes and amount of money available to the people who built them. The way that a synagogue is designed, and the things that are in it, are reminders of the **Temple** in Jerusalem. The architectural style of a synagogue generally follows the culture of the place where it is built. Whatever they look like, most synagogues have a Star of David outside, and there is usually **Hebrew** writing above the doorway. Inside, all synagogues are almost always built on a similar pattern.

Inside a synagogue

The Ark

At the front of the synagogue is a special cupboard or alcove called the Holy **Ark**. This is where the scrolls are kept when they are not being read. The scrolls are the most holy objects in the synagogue, and they are treated with great care. When the scroll is not being read, it is wrapped in a special cover sometimes called a **mantle**. These are often made of silk or velvet, but in some branches of Judaism covers are made of wood covered with silk. They are beautifully decorated. Covers are sometimes presented to the synagogue by someone wishing to celebrate a special event in their life, or to remember a relative who has died. The scrolls are also decorated with metal crowns and bells, attached to the end of the wooden rollers. These are also to remind people that the scrolls are special. Next to the Ark is a special seat for the **rabbi**, who leads the worship in the synagogue. There may be a similar seat at the other side of the Ark which can be used by visiting speakers.

◀ *Scrolls and their mantles in the Ark, the special cupboard where they are kept when they are not being read.*

Ner Tamid

Above the Ark is the **ner tamid**. This means 'continual light', and it is a light that never goes out. It is a reminder that God is always present. It is also a reminder of the lamp that burned in the Temple and never went out.

Bimah

The **bimah** is a raised platform. The **Torah** is read from this platform, so there is a table where the Torah can be laid while it is being read. The reader uses a special pointer called a **yad** to follow the words, because a Torah scroll should not be touched by hand. The person who is leading the service may stand on the bimah, or there may be a separate pulpit at the front of the synagogue.

Women's area

In **Orthodox** synagogues, it is not considered right for men and women to sit together. Women and young children sit in one area, men sit in another. The women's area may be a gallery upstairs or a separate section at the back. In other synagogues, everyone sits together.

Other areas

Ever since synagogues began, they have been used for other things as well as worship. In olden days, they often had rooms where Jews who were on a journey could stay. Today, there is usually a hall which can be used by members of the synagogue for wedding receptions or **Bar mitzvah** parties. It may also be used by the youth club, senior citizens group or any other group that the synagogue runs. There may also be smaller rooms used as classrooms which can be used for teaching children Hebrew.

▼ *Orthodox Jewish teenagers at a summer camp in the USA.*

David's view

David is 15 and lives in New York.

I enjoy going to **Temple**. Sometimes I go to the morning service with my father before he goes to work and I go to school. I know he finds it really helpful – he says that it's good to pray before you go off to work and to all the worries and stresses that a normal day brings. As well as the importance of the worship, I must admit that I still enjoy the feeling that I'm counted as a man, because that's only happened in the past couple of years since my Bar mitzvah. I like the festival services best, especially Simchat Torah where we get given candy at the end of the service! It's good that some of my friends from school go to the same Temple – it means we know a lot of the same people and it helps make us better buddies.

Major places of worship

The Temple

The **Temple** in Jerusalem was the most important place for Jews to worship God. It was the centre of their religion, and for hundreds of years Jews believed that it was the only place where they could worship God fully.

The first Jewish Temple was built by King Solomon in about 960 BCE. It took seven years to build and was magnificent. The Book of Chronicles describes Solomon's plans to build a Temple fit to worship God:

> I am building a Temple to honour the Lord my God. It will be a holy place where my people and I will worship him by burning incense of fragrant spices … Send me a man with skill in engraving, in working gold, silver, bronze and iron, and in making blue, purple and red cloth.
> (2 Chronicles 2: 4 and 7)

This Temple was destroyed when the Babylonians conquered the Jews' country in 586 BCE.

You can find the places mentioned in this book on the map on page 44.

The Second Temple

When Jews returned to Jerusalem, the Temple was rebuilt on the same site. Jews came from all over the world to worship there. They made sacrifices and listened to the **Torah** being read. The Temple was busiest on Mondays and Thursdays, which were market days in Jerusalem. The custom began of reading the Torah scrolls then as well as on Saturdays – the **Sabbath**. Today, the Torah is still read in synagogues on these days.

When Herod the Great became king in 39 BCE, he began rebuilding the Temple, and made it one of the most splendid buildings in the world. The outer walls were made of marble. Anyone could go into the outer courtyard, but only Jews were allowed into the second area. Only priests were allowed into the centre courtyard, where the Temple lamp was kept burning.

▼ After they had destroyed the temple in 70 CE, the Romans took its treasures to Rome, as shown in this relief from the Arch of Titus.

During the first century BCE, Palestine became part of the Roman Empire. In 66 CE, the Jews rebelled against Rome. The Romans crushed the rebellion. They entered the Temple and destroyed it. The whole place was burned and the Temple treasures were taken to Rome. The anniversary of the day on which the Temple was burned is a day of **fasting** for Jews, and is one of the saddest days of the Jewish year. **Orthodox** Jews still pray every day that the Temple will be restored. The only part of the Temple that survives is the Western Wall.

Keeping the memory of the Temple alive

Orthodox Jews hope and pray every day that one day the Temple will be restored. In the synagogue, prayers take place at the time sacrifices were offered in the Temple each day, and they always mention the Temple. At festivals, the readings from the Torah describe the Temple sacrifices offered at that festival. Whenever Orthodox Jews eat bread, they dip the first piece lightly in salt, to remember the salt that was sprinkled on the sacrifices. At the end of a Jewish wedding service, the groom breaks a glass under his foot to remind Jews that their joy can never be complete until the Temple is rebuilt.

The Touro synagogue

The Touro synagogue in Newport, Rhode Island is the oldest synagogue in the United States. It was built in 1759, and many people believe that it is one of the best examples of eighteenth-century architecture in the whole of America.

The synagogue was built of brick which was imported from England, and it stands at an acute angle to the street, so that the **Ark** can face Jerusalem and the site of the Temple. The women's gallery is supported by twelve columns, to remember the twelve tribes of Israel, and each one was made from a solid tree trunk. The congregation who began the synagogue had travelled to America to escape persecution in Europe, and there is a trapdoor under the **bimah**. This shows that even when the synagogue was built they were still afraid of attack.

Today, the synagogue is still a well-used place of worship, and it is visited by over 25,000 people every year.

▶ *America's oldest synagogue, in Newport, Rhode Island, showing the bimah and the women's gallery.*

Pilgrimage

A **pilgrimage** is a journey that someone makes because of their religion. It may involve going to the place where the religion began, or to somewhere that is important in its history. In the days of **Temple** worship, men were expected to make a pilgrimage there for the major festivals. Today, these festivals are celebrated at home, and Judaism does not require its followers to go on pilgrimages. However, Israel is a very important country for Jews, and many who do not live there aim to travel there not as tourists but as pilgrims.

You can find the places mentioned in this book on the map on page 44.

The Western Wall

The most important place of pilgrimage for Jews is in Jerusalem. It is called the Western Wall, and it is all that remains of the old Temple. Jews go there to pray, and to grieve for the loss of the Temple. They may carefully place small pieces of paper with prayers written on them into the spaces between the stones. Men and women pray separately. The sound of the prayers is the reason why non-Jews used to call the wall the Wailing Wall, but people now realize that this is insulting.

▼ *Prayers are carefully placed in the gaps in the Wall.*

Between the war that immediately followed the establishment of the state of Israel in 1948 and the Six-Day War in 1967, Jerusalem was divided in two. Jews lived in the west; Arabs lived in the east, which included the old city. This meant that no Jews could visit the remains of the Temple. As a result of the Six-Day War, Jews took control of the old city, and since that time daily services have been held at the Western Wall. The rest of the Temple site is occupied by a Muslim mosque, the Mosque of the Dome of the Rock.

▲ *The Western Wall is all that remains of the Temple built by Herod in 39 BCE, which was destroyed by the Romans in 70 CE.*

Yad Vashem

Another important place of pilgrimage for Jews is Yad Vashem. This is also in Jerusalem and covers 45 acres in an area called the Mount of Remembrance. Yad Vashem was set up in 1953 and is a combination of a shrine and exhibitions which are a memorial to the six million Jews who died in the **Holocaust**. Most Jews alive today know that members of their family were killed during World War II.

Yad Vashem has the largest library of information about the Holocaust in the world, with over 50 million pages of documents. It also holds hundreds of thousands of photographs and films. Some of these form part of the exhibitions. There are photographs of the **concentration camps** and the Jews who were imprisoned in them. There are displays of their clothing and other possessions.

Yad Vashem is made up of several different shrines, each intended to show a different aspect of the horror of the Holocaust. The Hall of Remembrance is a darkened room rather like a tent. It has a huge map. The names of death camps are engraved in **Hebrew** and English, and candles burn all the time, marking each one.

Part of the site is a Garden of the Righteous of the Nations, where trees and more recently a Wall of Honour commemorate non-Jewish men and women who risked their lives or their safety to rescue Jews. Names are still being added to this list which in 1999 had over 16,000 names on it.

In Israel, 27th Nisan (the seventh month of the Jewish year) is a day of remembrance for Jews who died in the Holocaust. This makes it a special day for people to visit Yad Vashem, though many Jews go there at other times, too.

Monument to a nation's grief

Abba Eban, an important Jewish politician at the time that Yad Vashem was begun, said:

'Yad Vashem is the monument to a nation's grief. It gives moving testimony to the unparalleled violence which afflicted the Jewish people at the hands of Nazi Germany, leaving a vast legacy of death and suffering in its wake. Yad Vashem is therefore one of the most significant landmarks in the moral history of mankind. It merits the reverence and support of free people everywhere.'

▼ *A sculpture at Yad Vashem.*

Festivals – Rosh Hashanah and Yom Kippur

Rosh Hashanah

Rosh Hashanah is the Jewish New Year. According to Jewish tradition, it is the anniversary of the beginning of the world – the day when God first created human beings. On the night before Rosh Hashanah, Jews eat a meal that includes apples dipped in honey. They say to each other, 'May it be the Lord's will to renew us for a year which will be good and sweet.' In other words, the apples and honey are a way of saying that they hope the coming year will be a pleasant one.

The shofar is made from a ram's horn.

At the synagogue service the following day, Jews offer each other good wishes for the new year. However, the service also has a more serious tone. It is the beginning of the most solemn time of the Jewish year, called the Days of Repentance or Returning. These are the days when Jews think about all the things they have done wrong during the past year. At the synagogue service Jews promise themselves and God that they will do better in the year to come. During the service, the **shofar** is blown. This is a sort of musical instrument made from a ram's horn. It plays two notes, and sounds a bit like a trumpet – very loud and solemn. The shofar is sounded one hundred times. Each time, Jews believe that it is reminding them to be sorry for all the things they have done wrong.

In some places, Jewish families meet after lunch on Rosh Hashanah and go for a walk. If there is a beach nearby, they will go there, otherwise they walk to a river. They empty crumbs from their pockets and throw them into the water. The way the crumbs are carried away by the water is a symbol of the Jews' hope that their sins will be forgiven.

The Days of Repentance

The Days of Repentance or Returning are the days between Rosh Hashanah and **Yom Kippur**, the **Day of Atonement**. During these ten days, Jews try to make sure that they put right everything that might be wrong in their life. For example, they try to make sure that they have made up any quarrels or arguments they have had, and that their life is all in order. This means that at the end of the ten days, they are ready to 'return' to God.

Yom Kippur

Yom Kippur means the Day of Atonement. Atonement means making up for something you have done wrong. Of course, Jews believe that they can pray to God for forgiveness at any time. However, Yom Kippur is a day set aside to ask God to forgive them for all the things they have done wrong. They can then become 'at one' with him. They believe that if they are really sorry for what they have done, and have made things right with other people, God will forgive them. This means that the day is also a time for celebrating God's goodness, and how much he loves them.

At Yom Kippur, Jews **fast** (go without food and drink) for 25 hours. This helps them concentrate on prayers. They spend a lot of the day at the synagogue. In the synagogue, the **Ark** and the reading desk are covered in white cloths, and the people leading the service wear white, too. This is a symbol of things being pure, and shows that they believe God will take away their sins. At the end of the Yom Kippur service, the shofar is blown again. This time its meaning is different from when it was blown at Rosh Hashanah. This time it reminds the people of all the good things they have promised themselves and God that they will do in the coming year.

The Jewish calendar

As well as using the calendar that is used by most people in Western countries, Jews have their own calendar. This has different months and a different numbering for the years, which go back to the creation, following the book of Genesis. The years begin in late September or early October, and are 3761 years ahead of the Western calendar. So, for example, autumn 2005 will be the start of the Jewish year 5766, 2010 the start of 5771, etc. Jewish months start at the new moon and last for 29 or 30 days. Festivals occur on fixed dates in these months. Every three years, an extra month is inserted into the calendar, so that the years keep pace with the 'solar years' on which the Western calendar is based.

Jewish month	Western equivalent
Tishrei	September/October
Cheshvan	October/November
Kislev	November/December
Tevet	December/January
Shevat	January/February
Adar	February/March
Nisan	March/April
Iyar	April/May
Sivan	May/June
Tammuz	June/July
Av	July/August
Ellul	August/September

Festivals – Pesach

Pesach (pronounced Pay'-sach, ch as in loch) is the Festival of Passover. It is the most important Jewish festival and it celebrates events that happened nearly 4000 years ago. The **Israelites** had been slaves in Egypt for hundreds of years, and Moses became sure that God wanted him to organize their release. The **Pharaoh** (Egyptian king) refused to let them go, because the work they were doing was very useful. Moses warned him that a series of disasters would hit the country. This came true, and after the tenth of these disasters – the death of the eldest son in every Egyptian house – the Pharaoh said that they really could go. The Israelites left immediately, without even waiting for the bread that they had been making for the journey to rise. Although he had said they could leave, the Pharaoh changed his mind soon after they had gone, and he sent his soldiers after them. The Israelites were saved when the water in the Sea of Reeds parted to allow them across, and then closed in again.

Jews remember these events in the festival of Passover every year. It lasts eight days and, for those eight days, Jews make sure that they do not come into contact with anything that contains leaven. Leaven is anything like yeast or self-raising flour that contains a raising agent. The house is searched carefully to make sure there are no crumbs hidden – down the sides of armchairs, for example. Nothing that contains leaven is eaten during the festival. Different bowls are used for washing up (or the sink is lined with tinfoil) and different crockery, cutlery and kitchen equipment is used for the festival. This is to make sure there is no trace of leaven anywhere near. Strictly **Orthodox** Jews will only eat foods which have been passed as '**kosher** for Passover'.

▲ 'Bedikat hametz' – searching for leaven.

The Seder

The **Seder** (pronounced Say-der) is a meal and it is the main part of the Passover celebrations. The meal follows a special order written down in a book called the Hagadah (pronounced Hag-a-dah' — sometimes spelt Haggadah). This tells how the Jews were slaves in Egypt, and how they escaped. The story is told as the meal is eaten. The youngest person at the meal asks four questions, and the oldest person answers them. The first question is 'Why is this night different from all other nights?' The questions and answers tell the story.

In the centre of the table is the Seder plate. This is divided into five sections, and has special foods on it. Other things on the table also have a symbolic meaning.

- A bowl of salt water is a symbol of the tears that the slaves cried.

- There is a glass of wine for each person. Wine is drunk four times during the meal, as a reminder that God promised four times he would free them.

- **Matzot** are 'cakes' of unleavened bread rather like flat crackers. They are a reminder of the bread that did not have time to rise before the Jews fled.

- A glass of wine for Elijah, one of the greatest **prophets** of Judaism. Jews believe that one day he will return to announce the coming of the **Messiah**.

The symbols on the Seder plate

Shank bone of lamb – not eaten, but a reminder of the lambs that were killed. The Israelites put lamb's blood above their doors so that the Angel of Death passed over them during the tenth plague. This gives the Passover festival its name.

Egg – hardboiled, then roasted in a flame – a symbol of new life.

Green vegetable – usually parsley or lettuce – a symbol of God's care for the Israelites.

Bitter herbs – usually horseradish – a reminder of the bitterness of slavery.

Charoset (pronounced Cha-ro'-set, ch as in loch) – a sweet mixture of nuts, apples, spices and wine. A reminder of the 'cement' used by the slaves when they were building, and of the sweetness of freedom.

▲ *The Seder plate contains five symbols for Passover.*

As well as the symbolic foods, the Seder includes a 'proper' meal. This may be anything that the family wishes to eat, and often includes chicken. After the meal, they usually stay at the table and sing songs. The traditional songs often have repeated words and choruses so that even very young children can enjoy joining in. The meal is a strong link with the Jews' history, and it looks forward to a time of peace and joy. The last words of the Seder are: 'Next year in Jerusalem, next year may all be free'.

Festivals – Sukkot

The second festival of the Jewish year is Sukkot, the Feast of **Tabernacles**. A tabernacle is a sort of hut or tent, and the **Hebrew** word for this is **sukkah** (plural sukkot). As part of their celebrations of the festival, Jews build a sukkah in the garden, and live in it for the week that the festival lasts. This is to remind them of the time after the **Israelites** had left Egypt and were travelling in the desert. For 40 years they had no fixed home. They lived in sukkot which they built when they reached an oasis, where they could find water. The other purpose of Sukkot is to be a reminder of the days when Jews used to take offerings of fruit to the **Temple** in Jerusalem.

A sukkah

A sukkah can be any size, but it must be large enough for at least one person to sit in. Sometimes Jews build a sukkah at the synagogue large enough for everyone who worships there to sit in. A sukkah must have at least three walls, but the most important part is the roof. This must be made of branches and leaves that are non-edible. It should be enough to provide shade, but not so thick that the sky cannot be seen. (For the same reason, a sukkah cannot be built under a tree or where a building hides the sky.) The roof is often decorated with fruit, and the sukkah may have other decorations in it.

▲ Some Jews build a sukkah for the whole synagogue congregation.

Sara's view

Sara is 14 and lives in Tel Aviv, Israel.

Sukkot is one of my favourite festivals. My brother and I make paper chains and other decorations to put in the sukkah and then we help to decorate it. We usually have little electric lights there, too. We use the garden shed, which has a roof we can lift off so that we can build the sukkah out of it every year. We eat our meals there, and sometimes we are allowed to camp out there at night. It makes it a real adventure. I like the idea that we are living in the same way as our ancestors did, thousands of years ago.

The lulav

At the synagogue services on each day of Sukkot (except Shabbat), Jewish men hold a **lulav**. This is a collection of branches from particular trees – palm, willow and myrtle. The branches are tied together and held in the right hand. In their left hand they hold a citron, a fruit similar to a lemon.

Each of these things is a symbol – something that has a deep meaning. The palm is a symbol of the spine. The willow is a symbol of the lips. The myrtle is a symbol of the eyes. The citron is a symbol of the heart. Holding the four things together is a symbol of the Jewish belief that God must be worshipped with every part of a person. During the synagogue services, one man stands on the **bimah** holding a **Torah** scroll. The other men walk around him holding the lulav. This is a reminder of how, in the days of the Temple, the people used to circle around the altar there. The lulav are also waved in all six directions, and back again towards the man's heart. This is a symbol that God is the ruler of all the universe.

Simchat Torah

The day after the end of Sukkot is called Simchat Torah. This means 'the Rejoicing of the Torah'. The books of the Torah are very important for Jews. Each week, parts of the books are read in the services in the synagogue. During the year, the five books are read all the way through. At Simchat Torah there is a special ceremony when the very last part of the Book of **Deuteronomy** is read, followed by the first part of the Book of **Genesis**. In this way, the readings start all over again. Jews believe that the books of the Torah tell how God wants them to live. Making sure that the readings go on without stopping is the way Jews show that they should never stop following what God wants.

Simchat Torah is a very joyful occasion. All the scrolls are taken out of **Ark** and are carried around the synagogue with the people dancing, singing and clapping after them. Children are often given sweets, chocolate and fruit as part of the celebrations.

▼ *Dancing around the synagogue at Simchat Torah.*

Festivals – Shavuot and Purim

Shavuot and Purim are festivals that celebrate events in the history of the Jews. Shavuot is a more important festival.

▲ *Decorating the synagogue for Shavuot.*

Shavuot

Shavuot is held seven weeks after Passover, so it is sometimes called the Feast of Weeks. It is the festival that celebrates God giving the Ten Commandments to Moses. Jews believe that this was the most important thing that has ever happened in the history of the world, because it was God explaining to people how he wanted them to live.

Before the festival begins, the synagogue is decorated with fruit and flowers. This is to remind people that, according to the **Torah**, Mount Sinai bloomed with flowers when God came down to give the Torah to Moses. At the synagogue service, there are readings from the holy books about how God gave the Ten Commandments to Moses. After the service, Jews celebrate with a meal at home. The meal includes two special loaves of bread with the pattern of a ladder baked into them. This is to remind people that Moses climbed the mountain to talk to God. Dairy foods are a traditional part of the Shavuot meal, too.

Purim

Purim is the story of King Xerxes and Queen Esther, king and queen of Persia (modern Iran) in the fifth century BCE, when many Jews lived there. Xerxes had a chief minister in the government called Haman, who was full of his own importance. He insisted that everyone should bow to him. Jews knew that bowing was a sign of worship, and it was wrong to worship anyone except God. One day, a Jew failed to bow as Haman walked past, and Haman became very angry. He decided to get rid of all the Jews in Persia. He went to Xerxes and told him that Jews were refusing to obey the laws of Persia. He persuaded the king to order that all Jews should be killed. Haman was superstitious, and he decided to draw lots to find out what would be the best day for the killing. Purim is a word for 'lots' and this gives the festival its name.

▼ *These girls are celebrating Purim.*

Queen Esther heard about Haman's plan. Although Xerxes did not know it, she was a Jew, and she decided she must try to save her people. However, the king was all-powerful, and she was only supposed to see him when he sent for her. She invited Xerxes and Haman to a feast. This was a very brave thing to do. Esther was obviously very frightened, because before she asked to see the king, she asked all Jews to **fast** and pray for three days and nights. During the feast she told the king the real reason for what Haman was planning – that it was because the Jews would not bow to him. Xerxes was very angry, and he ordered that Haman should be killed instead. All the Jews were saved.

The day before Purim is a day of fasting for Jews, to remember that Esther asked the Jews to fast and pray before she spoke to Xerxes. Then there is a synagogue service in which the story is read. During the reading, children stamp their feet and whistle every time the name of Haman is mentioned. Sometimes they use special rattles called greggors. The idea is to make as much noise as possible to drown out Haman's name. Children often take part in plays telling the story, and there are fancy dress parties. Purim is also a time for giving to charity, and people give each other presents of food.

Giving to charity

Giving to people who are less fortunate is an important part of Judaism. Giving to others is an important part of the festival of Purim, but Judaism teaches that giving charity should be done in a way that does not cause anyone embarrassment. At Purim, everyone, whether they are rich or poor, gives food to others. In this way, everyone can give and receive without feeling embarrassed. In Jewish teachings, there is a difference between giving money or gifts to other people, and giving of your time. Judaism teaches that if you are giving money it is better to give so that no one knows who has made the gift. Giving of your time and effort is very important in Jewish communities, and friends and neighbours generally help others if someone is ill, needs a babysitter, and so on.

Festivals – Hanukkah

Hanukkah is sometimes called the Festival of Lights. It falls in December (25th Kislev to 2nd Tevet) and it lasts for eight days. At Hanukkah Jews remember a story from their history.

The story of Hanukkah

The events that Jews remember at Hanukkah happened in Jerusalem almost 2000 years ago. A cruel emperor called Antiochus was ruling the Jews' country. He refused to let the Jews worship God. He said they had to worship him! The Jews knew that to worship someone who was only a man would break the most important of the Jewish commandments, which says that they must not worship anyone or anything but God.

▲ *Even very young children can enjoy joining in the festivals.*

A group of Jews decided to fight against Antiochus. They formed a guerrilla army who fought in secret against the soldiers of Antiochus. They were led by a man called Judah the Maccabee. Maccabee was his nickname – it is the **Hebrew** word for 'hammer'.

After three years of fighting, Judah and his friends captured Jerusalem. This meant they had gained control of the **Temple**, the most important building in the Jewish religion. Antiochus had wanted to make the Temple unfit for Jews to use for worship. He had ordered that a statue should be set up there, and that Jews should make sacrifices to it. Those who had refused had been tortured or killed. This idol-worship had made the Temple unclean. This means far more than just that it was dirty. It meant that the Jews could not use the Temple to worship God until it had been specially cleaned and made holy again.

When Judah was in control in Jerusalem, one of the first things he did was order that the Temple should be made a fit place in which to worship God again. This was obviously a difficult job – the stories say the Temple had been abandoned and grass was growing through the floor.

When it was ready, the Temple lamp was lit. This was a special lamp which was supposed to burn all the time, but Antiochus had let it go out. Judah and his friends found that there was only enough oil for it to burn for one night. The oil was special and it would take eight days to get more! But when the soldiers got back with the new oil, the lamp was still alight. The people said that it was a miracle. They believed that God had made the lamp stay alight to show how pleased he was that he could be worshipped in the Temple again. Judah and the soldiers also realized that this miracle showed that their victories had been miracles, too. Their tiny army had conquered Antiochus and all his soldiers, and they felt that they could only have achieved this with God's help.

▼ *Playing the dreidle game.*

Celebrating Hanukkah

In the celebrations for Hanukkah, Jews use a special candlestick called a hanukiah. It holds eight candles, plus another one called the servant candle or shamash. The shamash is used to light all the others. On the first night of the festival, Jewish families say special prayers and light the first candle. On the second night, they light two candles, and so on. By the end of the festival all nine candles burn brightly to show that the Jews are remembering the miracle of how the oil lasted. The hanukiah is often placed in the window, so that it can be seen clearly and gives light in the darkness. Although it is not one of the most important festivals, Hanukkah is a very happy time, especially for children. There are often parties and people give each other presents. They eat special foods such as doughnuts (fried in oil) and latkes, which are potato cakes fried in oil.

The dreidle game

There is a traditional game which Jewish children play at Hanukkah. It is called the dreidle game. A dreidle is like a spinning top with four flat sides or faces. On each side there is a Hebrew letter. They spell the first letters of the words which mean 'a great miracle happened here'. (Outside Israel, the last word is 'there' not 'here'.) The letters are Nun (ב) Hey (ח) Gimmel (ג) and Shin (ש).

When the game starts, there is a 'bank' of sweets or counters in the middle. If the dreidle falls on Nun, you do nothing. If it falls on Hey, you take half the sweets. If it falls on Gimmel, you take all of them. If it falls on Shin, you put sweets back in. Players add to the bank if it empties, and the game ends when a player taking all the sweets is declared the winner.

Family occasions – Bar mitzvah and Bat mitzvah

Bar mitzvah and Bat mitzvah are ceremonies held for Jewish boys and girls. Bar mitzvah takes place when a boy is thirteen. Bat mitzvah takes place when a girl is twelve or thirteen. After the ceremony the boy or girl is counted as a full member of the congregation of the synagogue.

Bar mitzvah

Bar mitzvah means 'son of the commandments'. On the Sabbath following his thirteenth birthday, a boy is called to the reading desk in the synagogue to recite the blessing on the Torah before it is read. Some boys read a part or even the whole of the sidra, the section of the Torah which is that day's reading. To read the Hebrew well enough to do this takes a lot of practice, especially when the boy is nervous at the idea of reading in front of lots of people. In many Orthodox synagogues, the boy will also have been given his own tefillin for the first time, and so he must learn how to put them on before the service.

After the boy has finished his reading, his father often gives a brief talk. In this he thanks God that the boy has grown up, and says that he is now counted as an adult. In some synagogues, the boy replies. Usually, the rabbi congratulates the boy too and gives a little talk for his benefit.

After the service, there is usually a celebration meal for the boy's family and friends who have come to the synagogue to support him. He is given presents, often books that will help him to learn more about Judaism. A popular gift is a Jewish prayer book, called a Siddur. Once he has become Bar mitzvah, a boy is counted as an adult in everything involving his religion. He can be counted as one of the minyan, the ten men who are necessary before a full synagogue service can be held, and he is expected to obey all of the Jewish laws.

▲ A Bar mitzvah celebration at the Western Wall.

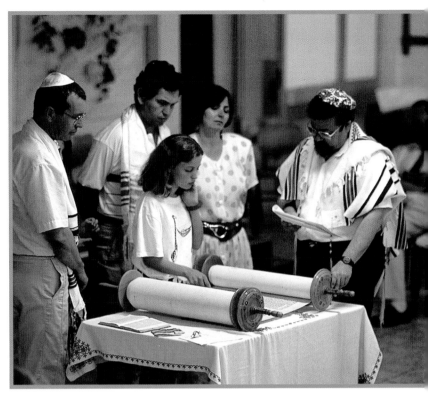

Bat mitzvah

Bat mitzvah means 'daughter of the commandments'. A girl becomes Bat mitzvah automatically at the age of twelve. Traditionally, Jewish girls did not have a celebration to mark their Bat mitzvah. Now, many Jews do have a celebration, but the form it takes can be very different in the different traditions. Orthodox synagogues that hold a service for girls hold it on a Sunday rather than on the Sabbath. Girls do not read from the Torah in an Orthodox synagogue.

In **Reform** and **Liberal** synagogues, there is no difference between the services held for boys and girls. There is usually a party for family and friends after the service.

Many synagogues hold **Bat chayil** ceremonies for girls. This means 'daughter of excellence'. Sometimes the girls prepare for the ceremony by learning more about Judaism and perhaps doing a project on some aspect of Judaism that particularly interests them. In the ceremony, the girls read a passage in Hebrew, and are welcomed by the congregation.

Jacob's view

Jacob is 13 and lives in Melbourne, Australia.

My Bar mitzvah was earlier this year. Of course, you know for years that when you get to thirteen you will become Bar mitzvah, and I was looking forward to it. But when it came to the Sabbath after my birthday, when I had to do the reading, I was scared stiff! The **Temple** was nearly full, and when I walked up to the reading desk I was really shaking. I was sure everyone could hear my heart beating. Then when I started reading everything was OK. I'd practised it a lot, and I knew everything really well, so I could just do it automatically. When I got to the end, I felt a bit flat – it was all over. Then we had the meal afterwards, and I got some great presents, so by the end I felt I'd had a really good day. Now I enjoy the feeling that I'm a full member of the congregation, and I can be one of the minyan. I don't find keeping all the Jewish laws that difficult at the moment, because we've always kept them at home, and I go to a Jewish school so I'm surrounded by people who live in the same way. Things might be a bit more difficult when I leave home, but being Jewish is so important to me that I can't see me ever changing that much.

Family occasions – marriage and death

Jews are expected to get married, and many Jews expect to marry other Jews. This is because being a Jew affects every part of your life. Many Jews believe that it is not really possible to share a life happily with someone who has not been brought up to follow the same faith and traditions. Others do not believe this is so important, and in the last 50 years increasing numbers of Jews have married 'outside' Judaism.

▲ *An outdoor wedding celebration in Israel.*

The marriage service

Jewish marriages usually take place in the synagogue, although they can be held in other places. In Israel, they are often held out of doors. The ceremony is conducted by a **rabbi**. In **Orthodox** communities, the couple **fast** until after the wedding service. They pray and ask forgiveness for things that they have done wrong. This is so that they can start the new stage of their life with a 'clean slate'.

Wherever the wedding takes place, the couple stand underneath a **huppah**. This is a special canopy which may be beautifully decorated with flowers. It is a symbol of the home that the couple will share. The service begins when the rabbi repeats a blessing over a cup of wine, then gives it to the bride and groom to drink. Then the **ketubah** is read. This is a marriage contract, in which the husband agrees that he will look after his wife. The bridegroom gives the bride a ring, which she wears on the first finger of her right hand. As he gives it to her he says 'With this ring you are sanctified to me according to the Law of Moses and Israel.' The rabbi then thanks God for creating human beings and for bringing happiness to the couple. At the end of the service, the groom breaks a glass by stepping on it. It is wrapped in paper to make sure that it does not do any damage. This is a very old custom and it has many meanings. It reminds the couple that there may be bad things as well as good things in their married life, and they must face them together. It is also a reminder of the destruction of the **Temple**.

As soon as the wedding service has ended, the bride and groom go into a separate room. They spend a few minutes together, and have something to eat if they have fasted before the service. Then they go back to the wedding guests for the rest of the celebrations. In olden days, and still in some traditional communities, the celebrations last a week. The bride and groom are invited to different people's homes every night to be the guests at a special meal.

Divorce

Jews allow divorce, but they usually go to great efforts to save a marriage. Friends and relations try to help the couple sort out their difficulties. If divorce cannot be avoided, a **get** must be issued. This is a certificate of divorce. It must be written on **parchment** by a trained scribe. It gives all the details of the couple, and of where and when they divorced. This is the only way that a Jewish marriage can be ended. A civil divorce (that is, one granted by a court of law) does not end a Jewish marriage, except in Israel, where the civil divorce is the Jewish divorce. Once the get has been issued, in Jewish law, either person is free to remarry.

Death

Jews believe that a funeral should take place soon after death, if possible within 24 hours. Men are usually buried wearing their **tallit**. Funerals are very simple, as Jews believe that rich and poor should be treated alike. Death happens to everyone. Jews do not normally allow cremation, as they believe it destroys what God has made. The time of formal mourning is called Shiva (seven), and lasts for a week. During this time the mourners do not leave home, and friends and members of the synagogue visit them three times every day to offer prayers and comfort them.

Jewish burial customs

Traditionally, the body of a Jewish person is prepared for burial by members of a *chevra kaddisha*. This is a 'burial society' which is made up of volunteers. Men prepare male bodies, and women prepare female ones. Preparing someone's body for burial is counted as a great responsibility. It is also seen as being the greatest kindness possible, because the person can never repay it. A Jew's body must not be buried wearing make-up or fine clothes. The body is washed, and wrapped in a plain linen shroud. Then it is placed in a plain wooden coffin. Rich and poor are treated in exactly the same way.

▶ *A Jewish cemetery on Mount Kidron, overlooking Jerusalem.*

What it means to be a Jew

The community

Many Jews choose to live in areas where there are other Jews. The rules about observing the **Sabbath** mean that a strict **Orthodox** Jew needs to live within a short walking distance of the synagogue. They need to attend Sabbath synagogue services, but they may not walk far, or drive a car or use public transport (because it involves other people working) on that day. Living in a community of Jews means that shops will cater for Jewish customers. There are likely to be specialist food shops, and supermarkets are more likely to sell **kosher** food. Most importantly, it enables Jews to mix with other Jews, people who share their religious traditions and ideas. Community groups are more likely – for example, many Jews like their children to spend at least some of their time with other young Jews, and playgroups or youth clubs can be important meeting places.

At the synagogue

Jewish men go to the synagogue as often as they can for the daily prayers. Attendance at Sabbath services and festivals is even more important. As well as the formal services, Jewish men and women often attend the synagogue for classes that teach them more about the **Torah** and about the way of life of Jews.

▲ *These Jews are meeting for study in the **rabbi's** home.*

In the home

Family life is important for Jews, and for many Jews their life at home is a very important part of their faith. The customs that they follow may have been handed down for generations. Being careful with the preparation of food – which they believe has been given by God – is a way of serving him. This is how the rules about kosher food fit into the pattern of life – not as rules which are there for the sake of it, but as a way of living which serves God.

Eating food, too, is a reason for thanking God, whom they believe has provided it, and many Jews recite special blessings for particular foods. For example, before eating fruit, they will say, 'Blessed are you O Lord our God, King of the universe, who creates the fruit of the tree.' For many Jews, blessing God in almost every situation in which they find themselves is so much a part of life that it is second nature.

▼ *Jews prepare food very carefully to make sure it is kosher (fit for Jews to eat).*

Keeping kosher

Kosher means 'allowed'. It is the way that Jews describe things that are fit and proper. Many Jews only eat kosher food. Anything that is not kosher is **treifah**, which means 'forbidden'. All plants are kosher, provided they do not have pests or 'creepy-crawlies' on or in them. Not all animals and birds are kosher. Animals that have a cloven hoof (that is, completely divided in two, like a cow's) and which chew the cud are kosher. Any others are not. Scavenger animals such as pigs are strictly forbidden. Some birds are allowed – Jews today eat chicken, turkey and duck. Fish are permitted if they have fins and scales.

To be kosher, an animal has to be killed by having its throat cut with a razor-sharp knife, so that it does not feel pain. The Torah forbids causing any animal to suffer. Meat must also be soaked in salt so that all blood is removed before it is cooked. Meat and dairy products are not eaten together. So, for example, they will not put butter on a meat sandwich or serve a pudding with custard after a meal that included meat. Jews have observed these rules for thousands of years. For Jews, careful preparation of food and thanking God for it by following the rules they believe he gave are an important part of their daily religion.

Map

The globe on the right shows the location of the map below.

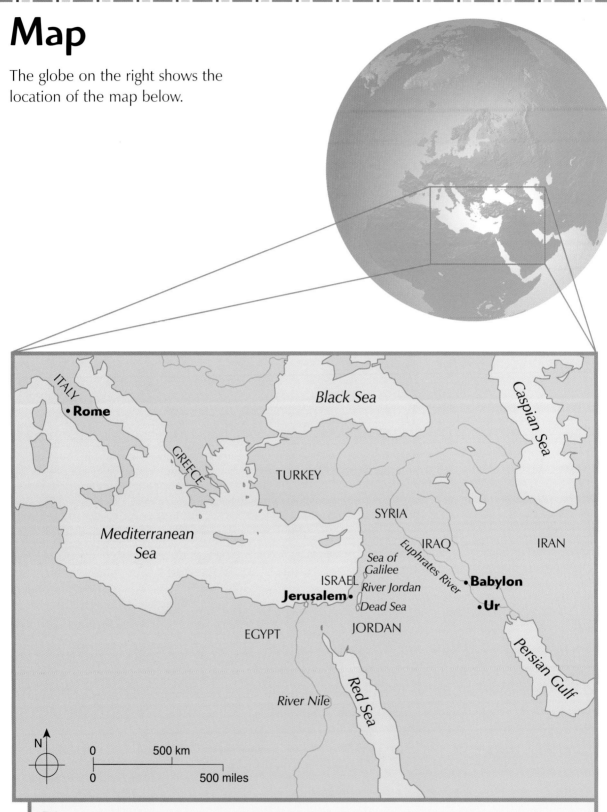

Place names

Some places on this map, or mentioned in the book, are called by different names today:

Assyria – ancient kingdom c1400–600 BCE centred around Northern Iraq and South East Turkey.

Babylon – ruins are 90 km south of Baghdad, Iraq

Babylonia – ancient region based around southern Iraq c1850 BCE–540 BCE

Palestine, Canaan – Israel

Persia – Iran

Ur – Tall-al-Maqayyar, Iraq.

Timechart

Major events in world history

BCE	3000–1700	Indus valley civilization flourished
	2500	Pyramids in Egypt built
	1800	Stonehenge completed
	1220	Ramses II builds the Temple of Amon (Egypt)
	1000	Nubian Empire (countries around the Nile) begins & lasts until c350 CE
	776	First Olympic games
	450s	Greece is a centre of art and literature under Pericles
	336–323	Conquests of Alexander the Great
	300	Mayan civilization begins
	200	Great Wall of China begun
	48	Julius Caesar becomes Roman Emperor
CE	79	Eruption of Vesuvius destroys Pompeii
	161–80	Golden Age of the Roman Empire under Marcus Aurelius
	330	Byzantine Empire begins
	868	First printed book (China)
	c1000	Leif Ericson may have discovered America
	1066	Battle of Hastings, Norman conquest of Britain
	1300	Ottoman Empire begins (lasts until 1922)
	1325	Aztec Empire begins (lasts until 1521)
	1400	Black Death kills one person in three throughout China, North Africa and Europe
	1452	Leonardo da Vinci born
	1492	Christopher Columbus sails to America
	1564	William Shakespeare born
	1620	Pilgrim Fathers arrive in what is now Massachusetts, USA
	1648	Taj Mahal built
	1768–71	Captain Cook sails to Australia
	1776	American Declaration of Independence
	1859	Charles Darwin publishes *Origin of Species*
	1908	Henry Ford produces the first Model T Ford car
	1914–18	World War I
	1929	Wall Street Crash and the Great Depression
	1939–45	World War II
	1946	First computer invented
	1953	Chemical structure of DNA discovered
	1969	First moon landings
	1981	AIDS virus diagnosed
	1984	Scientists discover a hole in the ozone layer
	1989	Berlin Wall is torn down
	1991	Break-up of the former Soviet Union
	1994	Nelson Mandela becomes President of South Africa
	1997	An adult mammal, Dolly the sheep, is cloned for the first time
	2000	Millennium celebrations take place all over the world

Major events in Jewish history

BCE	c2000	Life of Abraham, Jews call him 'our father Abraham'
	c1500	Life of Moses, who received the Ten Commandments on Mt. Sinai
	1500–1050	Time of the Judges – leaders of the twelve tribes of Israel
	1050	Saul becomes first king of Israel
	1002–970	Kingdom of David – united the country
	960	First Temple in Jerusalem built by King Solomon
	930	Division of kingdom into Israel and Judah
	722	Assyrians conquer Israel
	586	Babylonians conquer Judah and destroy first Temple, beginning of Diaspora
	538	Emperor Cyrus allows Jews to return to Jerusalem
	520–515	Temple rebuilt
	168	Revolt against Antiochus by Judah the Maccabee
	165	Temple is rededicated
	63	Roman conquest of Palestine
CE	70	Temple in Jerusalem destroyed by the Romans – only Western Wall remains
	200	The Mishnah – writings on important Jewish traditions – written down
	500	The Talmud – discussions by Jews about the Mishnah – collected and organized
	1200	Code of Maimonides written down
	1290	Jews expelled from England
	1492	Jews expelled from Spain
	1654	Jews begin to settle in New Amsterdam (New York) in the USA
	c1700–1760	Life of Baal Shem Tov, founder of Hasidism
	1818	First Reform synagogue (Hamburg temple)
	1841	First Reform Synagogue in United States opens
	1880s	Persecution in Russia and East European countries leads to mass migration, especially to USA
	1890s	Theodor Herzl begins Zionist movement, dedicated to founding a Jewish state in Israel
	1930s–40s	Persecution under Nazi rule and the Holocaust
	1948	Establishment of State of Israel
	1953	Yad Vashem, memorial to Jews killed in the Holocaust, established in Israel
	1967	Six-Day War unites Jerusalem under Israeli control
	1972	Reform movement ordains first woman rabbi
	1973	Yom Kippur War against Egypt and Syria
	1979	Peace treaty with Egypt
	1980	US National Holocaust Memorial Museum is chartered in Washington, D.C.
	1994	Peace treaty with Jordan.

Glossary

Adonai	'Lord' – Jewish name for God
adultery	sexual relations outside of marriage
Ark	special cupboard in the synagogue where scrolls are kept
Bar mitzvah	'son of the commandments' – ceremony for Jewish boys
Bat chayil	'daughter of excellence' – ceremony for Jewish girls
Bat mitzvah	'daughter of the commandments' – ceremony for Jewish girls
bet din	Jewish court
bimah	reading desk in a synagogue
challah	bread specially baked for the Sabbath
concentration camps	guarded prison camps where Nazis held millions of members of minority groups during World War II
convert	become a member of a religion
Covenant	solemn agreement (between God and the Jews)
covet	be jealous of what someone else owns
Day of Atonement	day on which Jews atone for their sins
Deuteronomy	fifth book of the Torah which includes the teaching Moses gave to the Israelites
Diaspora	name given to the spread of Jews around the world
eternal	lasting for ever
Exodus	second book of the Torah which includes the escape from Egypt and the time in the desert
fast	go without food and drink for religious reasons
Genesis	first book of the Torah which tells of the creation of the world and early Jewish history
get	certificate of Jewish divorce
Hasidim	Group of Orthodox Jews who follow strict laws about marriage, food, dress and religious life. The Hasidim tradition originated in Poland.
Havdalah	ceremony and prayers that end the Sabbath
Hebrew	traditional Jewish language. Modern Hebrew is the official language of Israel.
Holocaust	persecution of Jews during World War II
huppah	canopy under which Jewish weddings take place
idols	statues or false gods
Israelites	early name for the Jews
Judges	early leaders of the Jews
ketubah	marriage document
Ketuvim	'holy writings' – (third section of the Jewish holy books)
kippah	skullcap worn by many Jewish men
kosher	'fit' – food which Jews can eat
Leviticus	third book of the Torah, which tells us about Temple worship and festival observance

Liberal	branch of Judaism which began in Britain in the early twentieth century
lulav	branches used at Sukkot
mantle	decorative covering for scrolls
matzot	unleavened bread
menorah	seven-branched candlestick, similar to the lamp that burned in the Temple
Messiah	'promised one' who will come to establish God's kingdom.
mezuzah (plural **mezuzot**)	tiny scroll for placing on a doorpost
minyan	group of ten men, necessary for a full synagogue service
Mishnah	collection of the teachings of rabbis about the Torah
mitzvot	commandments – rules which Jews should follow
Nazis	members of the National Socialist Party, in power in Germany during the 1930s and 40s
ner tamid	everlasting light – a lamp in the synagogue
Nevi'im	(second section of the Jewish holy books) – the Books of the Prophets
Numbers	fourth book of the Torah which tells of counting the Israelites and some Jewish history
Orthodox	branch of Judaism whose members follow the Torah strictly
parchment	writing material made of animal skin
Pharaoh	Egyptian king
pilgrimage	journey for religious reasons
Progressive	'umbrella' term for non-Orthodox branches of Judaism
prophets	messengers from God
Psalms	part of the Jewish holy books
rabbi	Jewish teacher and leader
Reform	branch of Judaism begun in Germany in the eighteenth century
Sabbath	Jewish day of rest and worship
Seder	'order' – the Passover meal
Sefer Torah	Torah scroll
shofar	ram's horn instrument used in Jewish worship
shul	common name for synagogue
Siddur	Jewish prayer book
Sukkah (plural **Sukkot**)	a hut or tent used during the festival of Sukkot
Tabernacles	tents (Jewish festival)
tallit gadol	prayer robe used for worship
tallit katan	fringed garment worn under ordinary clothes
Talmud	collection of writings about Jewish law and teachings
tefillin (singular **tefillah**)	leather boxes worn by Orthodox Jewish men, usually for prayer
Temple	most important place of Jewish worship, destroyed by the Romans in 70 CE. Also used by Reform Jews In US for synagogue.
Tenakh	Jewish holy books
Torah	Books of Teaching – (first section of the Jewish holy books)
treif	forbidden (opposite of kosher)
yad	Hebrew word for 'hand' – pointer used when reading a Torah scroll

Index